Everything I Didn't Say © 2021 Morgan Wilson

Presentation by *BookLeaf Publishing*

Web: www.bookleafpub.com

E-mail: info@bookleafpub.com

ISBN: 9789358739268

First edition 2021

EVERYTHING I DIDN'T SAY

Morgan Wilson

BookLeaf Publishing

India | USA | UK

As always, for Mom. Love you to the Second Star to the Right and back.

And for you. You know who you are.

This is everything I didn't say…

for the past nineteen months.

maybe some of it will resonate with the person it is for.

and with you, the reader. Maybe you've had something you wanted to say after a breakup, but held it back, too. Maybe this will help you pull yourself together again and move on.

i'm rooting for you!

ACKNOWLEDGEMENTS

As always, writing it not a one-person job. I am the only one writing, true, but I without support, there's no way that I could have gotten anything done. Mom, thanks again for being my sounding board and rock in all things. I love you, and I can never repay you for all that you and Dad have done for me. Thank you for encouraging me to dig deep and write some of the most vulnerable pieces I have ever written, and for reminding me that you can be honest and sad without being bitter. Without you, I think I would have lost my mind.

 I'm not naming the inspiration for this poetry collection, but you know who you are. I do have to thank you, because without you, this would never have happened. You were the inspiration for every word, every poem here. I should also thank you for finally ending my writer's block. Thank you for both the good and bad times-yes, even the bad times.

I owe it all to God, my Almighty Father. He has given me the ability to put my feelings into words and has been with me every step of the way in my life. I do all that I do for Him.

Matthew 19:26

1. MISS ME

Do you miss me?

or are you just happy to be done with me?

Do you miss how much country music I played,

or how often I blasted the Jonas Brothers

or are you just happy you don't have to pretend to care?

Can you listen to Hunter Hayes anymore, or do you change the song?

Do you think of me when you see Kombucha at the store,

or are you just happy there's no one telling you to drink less soda?

Do you ever find yourself reaching out on instinct

to prevent someone from tripping?

Can you play that cooking game alone?

Or are you happy

that you don't have to check if someone is warm enough,

not tripping all over everything, or keeping track of constant migraines?

Or maybe it's the worst outcome of all.

When you're going about your day,

living your life,

maybe you don't think of me

at all.

2. RIGIIT

that new song "drivers license"

about the girl who drives around in the car crying

over a boy she isn't with anymore

and can't go to the places they used to

hits me freaking hard.

but there's a big difference between

her and I–

she has a right to be heartbroken

and I don't

but don't I?

don't I have a right

to drive down streets sobbing my eyes out

to pull over to the side of the road

because I'm sobbing so hard I can't breathe?

don't I have a right

to randomly start crying

in the middle of doing the dishes

because something, anything, reminded me of you?

don't I have a right to mourn

what I thought we had?

don't I have a right to be sad?

I broke up with you

but you broke my heart first.

3. WHAT IFS

Sometimes, I think I'm fully over you.

other times, I miss you so much still, that I can barely breathe,

can barely sleep,

can barely function.

pretty sad, huh?

they never told us that in the movies

where the dumper always ran off into the sunset

with the rest of their life

that you could be left with anger and regret

and sadness, just as much as the dumpee.

but newsflash: you can.

You weren't a bad boyfriend.

you weren't exactly great, towards the end.

but you were never a bad person.

I think that's what

has made this so hard for me.

you're a genuinely good person.

just not the right one for me.

That's what I have to keep reminding myself,

now that I'm back out in the dating scene-

not every guy is you,

without any ulterior motive

or games to play.

not everyone is as sweet, as caring as you were-

who gave so much of himself, without asking for anything back.

And sometimes I wonder,

deep in the corners of my mind, whispering:

what if I never find someone like you again?

4. FELL ASLEEP

I fell asleep listening to your voice last night,

from old videos I found.

(i don't even have old voicemails. how sad is that?)

Some were videos of the two of us, in better, simpler times

when things were happy.

I've never needed to fall asleep to the sound of your voice
before.

we've been broken up for almost two months, so why now?

I probably won't know the answer.

but it was a little bit of comfort.

5. SLEEP

I'm just so tired.

I worked 11 hours straight at work today!!! why!!

11 hours straight.

I miss having someone to text and have them ask "are you ok?"

especially if the answer is no.

And I know exactly what you would have said: "Go home, you do too much for them."

Even though you know I wouldn't have

because I care too much about other people.

Even at the expense of myself.

And I put way too much on myself.

And I would have liked to hear the nice things,

but what I would have liked more was

if you came to see me and held me until I fell asleep.

(do you remember when that was the only way that I could sleep?)

But we both know that you wouldn't have.

You didn't even do that when we were less than half an hour away from each other.

because you never would.

I want someone who would.

6. MISSING YOU

I can't really explain the knot that appears in my stomach
when i think of you.

maybe it's more like a hole in my heart,

where you used to be.

it's like a giant fist is squeezing my stomach,

and i get a lump in my throat

and i can't breathe;

sometimes when i think i'm fine,

it hits me like a sucker punch.

I used to wonder about you all the time

and i had no idea how to make it stop.

Maybe it's just hard for me to grasp

that i've cried myself to sleep from guilt

and you seem perfectly fine.

My mom says it's just because i can't go out on dates right
now,

but I don't think that's true.

I do miss you,

the hugs, the conversation, the way you laughed-

but as time passes, days slip into weeks, slip into months-

I'm starting to forget

why exactly

I missed

you

so

much.

7. 7 THINGS

The 7 things I hate about you:

you never paid for me??

refused to compromise,

only wore one (1) pair of tennis shoes,

say it with me: spontaneity!!

you dress like Adam Sandler,

never wanted variety

you were way too into anime

and you only wanted to see me on Saturday.

You don't get to hear the 7 things I like about you,

because you already did,

you heard fifty-two of them.

and you returned them.

8. "HEY, PRINCESS"

What if all the stars aligned?

Could I ever make you mine?

I don't care if it's only for a few days,

a few weeks,

a few months,

a few years.

It doesn't have to be forever.

I just want to know that I'll have

a little piece of you that'll be mine

Forever.

I don't even care if you break my heart.

For isn't it better

to have loved and have lost,

rather than to have never loved at all?

Do you still believe that? When you think of me?

9. "HEY, PRINCESS" PART 2

I wrote "hey princess" almost ten years ago in high school.

I don't know if I feel that way anymore.

Is it really better to have loved, and have lost?

You can't miss what you never had.

I thought I knew what that felt like back then,

But the truth is, I had never encountered real love or heartbreak.

For a while, I wondered if I've ever really had my heart broken

(In the present day).

How could I have, if I've never been broken up with?

(Not really)

But the truth is, you broke my heart so many times,

so many nights, over and over,

that I can say that I have experienced it.

The crying while driving home on a pitch-black freeway,

only illuminated by the headlights from other LA drivers,

the sobbing in the middle of Target in Westwood

(And not hiding it very well under my sunglasses).

I don't think I regret our relationship.

We had too many good moments for that to be entirely true.

But I don't think I agree that it's better to have loved and have lost,

because you can always miss what you once had.

And I think I always will.

10. COLORS

Roses are red, violets are blue,

Do you hate me? You promised not to.

Roses are red, grass is green,

How could you still be so mean?

Roses are red, clouds are grey,

You can't kiss my tears away.

Roses are red, docks are brown,

I felt like you were bringing me down.

Roses are red, flowers are pink,

Like the Titanic, we were a ship meant to sink.

Roses are red, doves are white,

I miss when we used to kiss all through the night.

Roses are red, your eyes are blue,

I hate that I still miss you.

11. FRIENDS & FOOLS

I genuinely thought that we would be if not friends, at least civil,

after the breakup.

I wasn't expecting us to be the kind of exes that can see each other on a regular basis,

hang out all the time, and stay in the same friend group

(We'd loved each other too much for that).

Remember when you said

something along the lines of 'not caring if I was the one who ended things,

because at least you would know what it was like to love someone fully?'

I do.

So when you ended up being extremely petty and bitter,

to the extent of sending me back my things via FedEX

(Like an empty pill bottle and gifts I hand made for you?

Harsh, by the way)?

With a typed letter, detailing all the ways I hurt you?

(We haven't spoken since)

I was more hurt than I thought I would be.

I guess I thought you were a bigger person than you actually
are.

But we already knew I was a fool.

12. THE VILLAIN OF THE STORY

I thought that if I called you,

crying and saying that I made a mistake, and I wanted you back,

that you would take me back,

no questions asked.

but now, I'm not so sure.

You seem to be fine-just-fine,

Posting stupid streaming videos one day,

And liberal political takes the other.

Even making a so-called "comedy" video about a waiter on Valentine's Day.

(to which I say: "REALLY?")

It's like you're deliberately doing things I can't stand.

It's ironic

that I'm the one who ended the relationship,

yet I'm the one

stuck in memories

while you're moving on.

It's ironic

that I'm the one who did what was best

for the both of us–

Yet I'm the villain of the story.

But isn't that always how it is?

History is written by the winners

And only time will tell which one of us that is.

13. WHAT WILL YOU TELL HER?

It's practically gospel that once your relationship is over,

your ex becomes joke fodder.

No matter how you broke up,

it's almost human nature.

I never really thought about it before,

but do you make fun of me now?

Do you sit with my old roommates and laugh

about things you used to love me for?

Is my enthusiasm for Scooby-Doo now "childish?"

Is the way I would cry at movies pathetic,

my love for books now nerdy,

my way of saying "y'all" weird instead of quirky?

I wonder how I'll be described to your next girlfriend.

You were always careful to be polite in the past,

but I can't help but wonder

if I'll get that courtesy.

How will your friends describe me to her?

A wreck? dramatic? too Disney-obsessed? too innocent?

A walking disaster? anti-confrontational?

Definitely liked stuffed animals way too much for someone my age?

(if you don't like stuffed animals, I don't like you)

On a more serious level, what will you say about me?

That I broke your heart without warning?

That I hid my true feelings,

and acted like everything was fine,

only to rip the rug out from underneath you and let you crash to the floor?

Or will you tell her good things?

That I was your number one supporter,

I was fiercely protective, too caring for my own good,

that I loved giving hugs and laughed at all your jokes?

Will you tell her that I did try really hard, at everything?

That we'd begun to plan our lives together?

Will you tell her that I was scared you would leave, but I was the one that did?

Sometimes it keeps me up at night.

14. ALONE

sometimes it keeps me up at night,

that I used to cry and tell you,

with tears streaming down my face,

that I was scared one day, you'd be tired of dealing with me-

the long distance, my migraines, depression thanks to the
state of the world,

just the constant stress I was under-

and you would leave me.

and you would always tell me no.

you'd never leave me, ever.

you loved me so much.

and for that moment, in your arms, I felt safe.

Do you remember the night that we decided to watch *Rise of
the Guardians*

because I couldn't believe you hadn't seen it yet?

I'd bought a bottle of wine at Target that day

which was pretty normal, and I had a glass to start.

when we were together, I never saw you drink much.

that night was no exception, no big deal.

we'd watched so many movies together, I'd lost count.

a major theme in *Rise* is the question:

 "What's your biggest fear?"

we all have them-even Santa, the Easter Bunny, and the
unflappable Jack Frost,

or so the movie says.

Pitch, the boogeyman, asks Jack,

"What do you fear the most?"

I turned to you, about four glasses in at this point, and asked
you-

I'm a little ashamed to say that I don't remember your
response

but I do remember that mine made me cry:

being alone.
this seemed to startle you, although I'm not sure

if it was the tears or the answer that did it

but it's kind of sad, isn't it,

that I wasn't physically or emotionally alone

I felt like I was.

that was right before Christmas,

when I was struggling to hold on to you-

struggling to hold on to us

struggling to hold onto the girl I'd been a year ago when we'd started dating.

I think I cried a lot, my memories are fuzzy.

my tears made you cry, too

and I remember being touched that you were a sympathy crier

but also could feel my heart cracking in two

because YOU were part of the reason why I felt so alone.

I blamed my tears on the wine, stress, the movie-

And you'd followed my lead.

I wonder what would have happened if you hadn't.

15. LONELY

Dating you was lonely.

it just hit me today,

like someone had smacked me over the head with one of my own heavy books.

dating you, I'd always be second to your career.

I should have known it from the beginning.

when on our third date

I had to make my own friends

because you got selected to be a character in the murder mystery dinner.

I mean, really?

I knew completely no one, and even for an extrovert, that's a lot.

but it was still the beginning,

and that was the night I started to fall in love

with the boy that would drive from LA to the beach and back

just to take me to a party.

but when we'd been dating for months, and sometimes I

wouldn't hear

from you until 2 or 3 in the afternoon

when even a "good morning, gonna be busy today"

message would have been nice.

It was like you'd done everything you could to get me

and then had given up altogether.

I should have known from the start.

16. I WANT YOU TO BE HAPPY

I want you to be happy.

really, I do.

I know, you're probably rolling your eyes and scoffing at me.

How could I want you to be happy,

when I selfishly broke your heart?

that's why I did it.

Because I wouldn't make you happy,

not really.

not long term.

I worry about you.

Sometimes I check on you via my work social media,

because I haven't blocked you on there,

and it makes my heart hurt.

Everything you post, big and small,

from the work insta stories to the tagged photos.

I used to know almost everything.

And now I know nothing.

I desperately want you to be healthy and happy.

Get a six-pack, get jacked.

Get all the acting jobs you want,

guest star on Smosh,

become famous to the point where I have to avoid your face
on billboards-

I really do want you to achieve your dreams.

Hell, even find someone else and get married-

I don't even care if she's prettier than me-ok, that's a lie. I'm
not a saint.

but she can be ALMOST as pretty as me.

(I'll give you that much.)

But I still wish you the best.

That you become closer with your family,

that you get all the cats you want,

that you get a job you love,

that you're so unbelievably happy

you forget about the girl who sobbed in the foyer

of the crappy house you rented

while she broke your heart.

That you barely even remember what I put you through.

That you have no reason to remember.

Living your best life possible.

Do you wish the same for me?

17. WHAT IF NO ONE ELSE WILL LOVE YOU?

My mom says that I still spend so much time

reflecting

because of the state of the world,

that as soon as I can go out and meet someone

I'll forget all about you.

that I'm just romanticizing and remembering the good parts

because I don't have anyone else.

but I don't think that's necessarily true.

we were together for a long time,

and for most of that time, we were a huge part of each other's lives

especially during those months when I could only see about half a dozen people

and you, even less.

and now, trying to date again,

I'm exhausted.

I simply do not have the energy to do this again.

the second-guessing, and the intro questions, and constantly trying to be someone I'm not.

I've got a little voice in the back of my head that asks

"What if he was the best you could do, and now you'll be alone forever?"

maybe no one will love me like you did.

"what if no one else will love you?"

and that terrifies me.

18. THINKING

Did you think, when I kissed you for the first time

in one of the many parking lots by the Staples Center,

at the end of our first date,

that I would break your heart?

did you think that I would mean so much to you?

did you think that you would mean so much to me, and I'd do
it anyway?

I didn't.

sometimes I still see

a little boy with curly dirty blonde hair and blue eyes,

and the cutest dimples you've ever seen,

who has me wrapped around his finger,

and my chest hurts so much I can barely breathe.

I can still picture you coming home from work or a shoot,

smiling at me with laugh lines and grey in your hair.

so why did it have to go away?

why did you have to love performing for people

more

than

me?

19. Y?

If you loved me so much,

why did you let me go without a fight?

if you knew I was upset with you

why didn't you do more?

texting "are you mad at me" does not count.

why didn't you try harder

when I came to break up with you?

why did you let me go so easily?

If you "knew it was coming?"

why?

are you already glad to be rid of me

or will I always be the one that got away?

the one in the back of your head

that you'll always wonder about, just a little?

I wonder how long it's going to take

for me to get over

what we could have had.

20. read about

I want what I read about

the guy that will do anything to keep the girl

the guy who loves her so much he can't consider letting her
go

who always puts in effort

does things just to make her happy

actually reciprocates one damn time.

maybe I expected too much.

maybe be I'm too much of a burden,

and you're happy to be done with me.

you're relieved to not have to deal with

my dramatics and my stress.

it's not like I can call you up and ask you.

it haunts me that I'll never know.

www.ingramcontent.com/pod-product-compliance
Lightning Source LLC
LaVergne TN
LVHW051238200726